Comptroller of the Currency
Administrator of National Banks

Internal Control

Comptroller's Handbook

January 2001

Management

Internal Control

Table of Contents

Overview

Background

Effective internal controls are the foundation of safe and sound banking. A properly designed and consistently enforced system of operational and financial internal control helps a bank's board of directors and management safeguard the bank's resources, produce reliable financial reports, and comply with laws and regulations. Effective internal control also reduces the possibility of significant errors and irregularities and assists in their timely detection when they do occur.

A bank's board of directors and senior management cannot delegate their responsibilities for establishing, maintaining, and operating an effective system of internal control. The board must ensure that senior management regularly verifies the integrity of the bank's internal control.

Although internal control and internal audit are closely related, they are distinct from each other. Internal control is the systems, policies, procedures, and processes effected by the board of directors, management, and other personnel to safeguard bank assets, limit or control risks, and achieve a bank's objectives. Internal audit provides an objective, independent review of bank activities, internal controls, and management information systems to help the board and management monitor and evaluate internal control adequacy and effectiveness.

OCC examiners will assess and draw conclusions about the adequacy of a bank's internal control during every supervisory cycle. This assessment will include validation, including some level of verification or testing, when necessary.

This booklet discusses the characteristics of effective controls and will help examiners and bankers assess the quality and effectiveness of internal control. It also describes OCC's supervisory process for internal control reviews and the roles and responsibilities of the board of directors and management.

This booklet supplements the basic guidance in the "Large Bank Supervision" and the "Community Bank Supervision" booklets of the Comptroller's Handbook. Further guidance on assessing controls for specific examination areas or banking products, business lines, and activities can be found in the associated Comptroller's Handbook booklets.

Internal Control Objectives

Effective internal control provides bankers and examiners reasonable assurance that

- Bank operations are efficient and effective.
- Recorded transactions are accurate.
- Financial reporting is reliable.
- Risk management systems are effective.
- The bank complies with banking laws and regulations, internal policies, and internal procedures.

Control systems can help bank managers measure performance, make decisions, evaluate processes, and limit risks. Good internal control can help a bank achieve its objectives and avoid surprises. Effective control systems may detect mistakes caused by personal distraction, carelessness, fatigue, errors in judgment, or unclear instructions in addition to fraud or deliberate noncompliance with policies. Effective and well-designed control systems are still subject to execution risk. In other words, human beings still must execute most control systems and even well trained personnel with the best of intentions can become distracted, careless, tired, or confused.

Internal control must be consistently applied and well understood by bank staff if board and management policies are to be effectively implemented. Controls typically (1) limit authorities, (2) safeguard access to and use of records and bank assets, (3) separate and rotate duties, and (4) ensure both regular and unscheduled reviews, including testing.

Regulatory Requirements

National banks must adhere to certain regulatory requirements regarding internal control. These requirements direct banks to operate in a safe and sound manner, accurately prepare their financial statements, and comply with other banking laws and regulations. The laws and regulations that establish minimum requirements for internal control are 12 CFR 30, Safety and Soundness Standards; 12 CFR 363, Annual Independent Audits and Reporting Requirements; and 15 USC 78m, Securities Exchange Act of 1934.

12 CFR 30

12 CFR 30, Safety and Soundness Standards, establishes certain managerial and operational standards for all insured national banks, including standards for internal control. Appendix A to 12 CFR 30 states that a national bank should have internal controls that are appropriate to the size of the bank and the nature, scope, and risk of its activities, and that provide for

- An organizational structure that establishes clear lines of authority and responsibility for monitoring adherence to prescribed policies.

- Effective risk assessment.

- Timely and accurate financial, operational, and regulatory reports.

- Adequate procedures to safeguard and manage assets.

- Compliance with applicable laws and regulations.

When a national bank fails to meet these standards, the OCC may require management to submit a compliance plan to address internal control deficiencies. If the bank fails to submit a satisfactory plan, the OCC must, by order, require the bank to correct the deficiency.

12 CFR 363

12 CFR 363, Annual Independent Audits and Reporting Requirements, applies to national banks having total assets of $500 million or more.

Covered national banks must submit an annual report to their OCC supervisory office and the FDIC. The annual report must include

- A report containing

  - Annual audited financial statements.

  - A statement of management's responsibilities for preparing financial statements, establishing and maintaining internal control and procedures for financial reporting, and complying with safety and soundness laws concerning loans to insiders and dividend restrictions.

  - Management's assessment of the effectiveness of the bank's internal control and procedures for financial reporting as of the end of the fiscal year, and management's assessment of the bank's compliance with designated laws and regulations during the most recent fiscal year.

- A report by the independent public accountant attesting to management's assertions regarding internal control and procedures for financial reporting.

15 USC 78m

15 USC 78m, Securities Exchange Act of 1934, requires banks and holding companies with a class of securities registered pursuant to the Securities Exchange Act of 1934 to develop and maintain a system of internal accounting controls. For registered banks/holding companies, such controls should ensure that

- Transactions are executed in accordance with management's general or specific authorization.

- Transactions are recorded to permit preparation of financial statements in conformance with generally accepted accounting principles or any other criteria applicable to such statements, and to maintain accountability for assets.

- Access to assets is permitted only in accordance with management's general or specific authorization.

- Accounting records on assets are compared with the assets at reasonable intervals and appropriate action is taken to reconcile any differences.

Internal Control Components

The formality of any control system will depend largely on a bank's size, the complexity of its operations, and its risk profile. Less formal and structured internal control systems at community banks can be as effective as more formal and structured internal control systems at larger and more complex banks. Every effective control system should have[1]

- A control environment.
- Risk assessment.
- Control activities.
- Accounting, information, and communication systems.
- Self-assessment or monitoring.

The control environment reflects the board of directors' and management's commitment to internal control. It provides discipline and structure to the control system. Elements of the control environment include

- The organizational structure of the institution. (Is the bank's organization centralized or decentralized? Are authorities and responsibilities clear? Are reporting relationships well designed?)

- Management's philosophy and operating style. (Are the bank's business strategies formal or informal? Is its philosophy and operating style conservative or aggressive? Have its risk strategies been successful?)

---

[1] The Committee of Sponsoring Organizations of the Treadway Commission (COSO)1992 report "Internal Control – Integrated Framework" discusses control system structures and components. COSO is a voluntary private-sector organization, formed in 1985, dedicated to improving the quality of financial reporting through business ethics, effective internal control, and corporate governance. The American Accounting Association, the American Institute of Certified Public Accountants, the Financial Executives Institute, the Institute of Internal Auditors, and the National Association of Accountants (now the Institute of Management Accountants) jointly sponsored the National Commission.

- The integrity, ethics, and competence of personnel.

- The external influences that affect the bank's operations and risk management practices (e.g., independent audits).

- The attention and direction provided by the board of directors and its committees, especially the audit or risk management committees.

- The effectiveness of human resources policies and procedures.

Risk assessment is the identification, measurement, and analysis of risks, both internal and external, controllable and uncontrollable, at individual business levels and for the bank as a whole. Management must assess all risks facing the bank because uncontrolled risk-taking can prevent the bank from reaching its objectives or can jeopardize its operations. Effective risk assessments help determine what the risks are, what controls are needed, and how they should be managed.

Control activities are the policies, procedures, and practices established to help ensure that bank personnel carry out board and management directives at every business level throughout the bank. These activities help ensure that the board and management act to control risks that could prevent a bank from attaining its objectives. They should include

- Reviews of operating performance and exception reports. For example, senior management regularly should review reports showing financial results to date versus budget amounts, and the loan department manager should review weekly reports on delinquencies or documentation exceptions.

- Approvals and authorization for transactions and activities. For example, an appropriate level of management should approve and authorize all transactions over a specified limit, and authorization should require dual signatures.

- Segregation of duties to reduce a person's opportunity to commit and conceal fraud or errors. For example, assets should not be in the custody of the person who authorizes or records transactions.

- The requirement that officers and employees in sensitive positions be absent for two consecutive weeks each year.

- Design and use of documents and records to help ensure that transactions and events are recorded. For example, using pre-numbered documents facilitates monitoring.

- Safeguards for access to and use of assets and records. To safeguard data processing areas, for example, a bank should secure facilities and control access to computer programs and data files.

- Independent checks on whether jobs are getting done and recorded amounts are accurate. Examples of independent checks include account reconciliation, computer-programmed controls, management review of reports that summarize account balances, and user review of computer-generated reports.

Banks are required to develop and maintain written procedures or controls for certain areas, including real estate lending, asset management, and emerging market and trading activities, as well as areas subject to insider transactions, the Bank Secrecy Act, and the Bank Bribery Statute. Although the OCC encourages banks to have written internal control procedures in all areas, having them is not enough. Personnel must understand control procedures and follow them conscientiously.

Accounting, information, and communication systems capture and impart pertinent and timely information in a form that enables the board, management, and employees to carry out their responsibilities. Accounting systems are the methods and records that identify, assemble, analyze, classify, record, and report a bank's transactions. Information and communication systems enable all personnel to understand their roles in the control system, how their roles relate to others, and their accountability. Information systems produce reports on operations, finance, and compliance that enable management and the board to run the bank. Communication systems impart information throughout the bank and to external parties such as regulators, examiners, shareholders, and customers.

Self-assessment or monitoring is the bank's own oversight of the control system's performance. Self-assessments are evaluations of departmental or operational controls by persons within the area. Ongoing monitoring should be part of the normal course of daily operations and activities. Internal and external audit functions, as part of the monitoring system, may provide independent assessments of the quality and effectiveness of a control system's design and performance. All bank personnel should share responsibility for self-assessment or monitoring; everyone should understand his or her responsibility to report any breaches of the control system.

Strong control cultures typically incorporate qualified personnel, effective risk identification and analysis, clear designation and appropriate separation of responsibilities, accurate and timely information flow, and established monitoring and follow-up processes. For example, the lending area should have (1) a board of directors active in approving and monitoring loan policies and practices; (2) a loan review function that evaluates the risk and quality of loan portfolios; (3) policies and procedures governing, among other things, types of loans, loan approvals, maturity limits, rate structure, and collateral requirements; and (4) information systems that allow for proper management and monitoring of the lending area.

OCC Internal Control Supervision

Evaluating internal control is fundamental to the OCC's overall supervisory process. OCC's internal control assessments, along with its assessments of the bank's audit programs, help leverage OCC resources, establish the scopes of other examination activities, and contribute to developing strategies for future supervisory activities. Examiners will base the scope, type, and depth of an internal control review on the bank's size, complexity, scope of activities, and risk profile, as well as on the OCC's assessment of the bank's audit functions.

Supervisory Principles

When reviewing a bank's internal controls, examiners should remember the following:

Integration. Examiners should integrate and coordinate internal control reviews with the supervisory activities for other examination areas, especially the audit area. Core assessment standards and other tools, such as internal control questionnaires (ICQs) and the sample CEO questionnaire in appendix A, can help examiners assess and document conclusions about individual examination areas. These tools also help examiners incorporate their findings and conclusions into an overall internal control assessment.

Analysis. Examiners review and analyze available information to identify systemic control issues, to gauge changes in the bank's control environment and overall risk profile, and to evaluate controls in general. Useful sources of information include management discussions, organization charts, procedural manuals, operating instructions, job specifications and descriptions, directives to employees, flow charts, operating losses incurred by the bank, and internal and external audit reports, management letters, and other control and risk assessment material. These materials will assist examiners in reviewing the bank's operating systems and procedures.

Communication. OCC staff will maintain ongoing and clear communications with bank personnel. In large banks, the examiner-in-charge (EIC) or designee should have periodic meetings with bank personnel or committees closely associated with risk control functions (e.g., audit or risk committees, risk managers, control officers, auditors). While this degree of contact may not be practical for all community banks, meetings with control personnel should occur as frequently as necessary. Communication regarding OCC's internal control supervision and findings should occur throughout an examination or supervisory cycle. Examination reports and other written communications to a bank will include comments about the adequacy of the bank's control functions and summarize other appropriate findings and conclusions.

Linkage. The quality and reliability of a bank's internal control function are factors in CAMELS ratings (especially for the management component) and ratings of specialty areas (i.e., information systems, consumer compliance, and asset management). Examiners will also incorporate findings about internal control adequacy in the OCC's risk assessments.

Documentation. Examiners should prepare documentation in the form of work papers, according to PPM 5400-8, "Examination Work Papers." Work papers, which may be in paper or electronic form, must contain essential information to support conclusions about the evaluation of internal control. The level of detail should be commensurate with the risks facing the institution and provide an audit trail that supports examination conclusions. The examiner should generate and retain only those documents necessary to support the scope of the review, significant conclusions, ratings changes, or changes in risk profile. Examiners can reproduce or excerpt readily available bank information and incorporate the information in the examination work papers to avoid duplication of effort.

Supervisory Process and Validation

During every supervisory cycle, OCC examiners will assess the adequacy of a bank's internal control as strong, satisfactory, or weak. Examiners should begin their control assessment by reviewing the work of the bank's internal audit or other control review functions, generally as part of pre-examination planning. Examiners should make a preliminary assessment of internal control reliability and identify control problems, areas of potential or high risk, and areas not recently reviewed. That assessment will influence how much validation work examiners will perform during onsite supervisory activities.

Validation encompasses inquiry, observation, and testing as appropriate, of the bank's control systems. Examiners should coordinate control validation with examiners responsible for other examination areas. How thoroughly an examiner validates internal control for a specific examination area depends on how much supervisory concern he or she has about that area. Generally, examiners begin with a discussion with a bank's chief executive officer (CEO) or other person responsible for control management to gain an overall understanding of and insight into the bank's control system. As warranted, examiners perform independent verification or testing of internal control integrity if substantive issues surface that raise questions about the adequacy or effectiveness of the control systems.[2]

Examiners will use the internal control core assessment objectives and procedures from the "Community Bank Supervision" and "Large Bank Supervision" booklets of the Comptroller's Handbook as the starting point in scoping control examination work. Examiners may supplement those core assessment procedures with the more detailed expanded procedures in this booklet, the "Internal and External Audits" section, and other Comptroller's Handbook sections on specific banking activities. Examiners should use judgment to decide when to use the procedures in this and other booklets. In making this judgment, the examiner should consider the bank's size, complexity, scope of activities, history of control issues, and risk profile, including the quantity of risk and the quality of risk management.

Internal Control Evaluation

Evaluating internal control involves (1) identifying the internal control objectives relevant to the bank, department, business line, or product[3]; (2) reviewing pertinent policies, procedures, and documentation; (3) discussing controls with appropriate levels of bank personnel; (4) observing the control environment; (5) testing transactions as appropriate; (6) sharing findings, concerns, and recommendations with the board of directors and senior management; and (7) determining that the bank has taken timely corrective action on noted deficiencies. For banks subject to 12 CFR 363, documentation associated with their internal control assessment should provide examiners an excellent resource in determining whether bank

---

[2] Examiners can find additional guidance for securing access to bank information and records to confirm the existence of bank assets in PPM 5310-10 "Guidance to Examiners in Securing Access to Bank Books and Records."

[3] Examiners should evaluate the consolidated risk profile of the national bank, including the potential material risk posed by functionally regulated activities conducted by the bank or functionally regulated subsidiaries or affiliates. For functionally regulated activities, examiners should focus on the effectiveness of bank systems for monitoring and controlling operational and financial risks, intercompany transactions, and compliance with laws under OCC specific jurisdiction. Examiners can obtain much of this information during routine meetings with bank management. Examiners can access additional guidance on OCC examination of functionally regulated activities and entities on OCCnet's financial modernization homepage.

management performs a satisfactory assessment of the bank's control structure.

In reviewing internal control in a specific area of the bank, an examiner should identify key control personnel and positions by asking the following questions:

- Is this a critical position? Can a person in this position make a significant error that will result in the inaccurate recording of transactions? Can he or she enter false information or gain control of assets?

- If an error or irregularity occurs, would normal controls promptly disclose it? Would controls prevent or detect significant errors or irregularities?

- Is it possible for a person to conceal an error or irregularity, and are there controls in place to minimize this possibility?

Primarily, the examiner's concern is with bank personnel who have influence over financial records and access to assets. Persons in these positions could be involved in information processing (computer programmers) or investment and trading activities (traders, buyers, and sellers). Once those positions have been identified, the examiner must determine whether internal controls will either prevent errors and irregularities or uncover them promptly. One example of such controls is the requirement that employees in key or influential positions be absent two consecutive weeks each year.

Examiners should ensure that employee duties and responsibilities are properly segregated to minimize the possibility of errors and irregularities. For example, in the investment area, the following duties should be strictly segregated: executing securities transactions, approving transactions, accessing securities record keeping, and posting or reconciling related accounting records. Examiners should investigate any activity in which controls do not prevent persons from having both custody and record keeping responsibilities for bank assets and determine whether mitigating factors exist. Segregation of duties can break down when controls do not keep pace with a bank's growth and diversification, practices become lax, or personnel use their knowledge or influence to circumvent control.

Before reaching conclusions about a specific area's internal control, examiners must consider circumstances that may cause bank employees or officers to take undue risks. The examiner should be especially alert to circumstances in which the personal financial interests of key officers or employees depend directly on the financial condition of the bank. Sound internal control ensures that conflicts of interest are minimized or controlled. Both manifest and potential conflicts of interest should be considered in the overall assessment of internal control.[4]

In addition, the examiner should be alert to deviations by bank personnel from established policies, practices, and procedures. Such deviations may exist when

- Instructions and directives are not reviewed and revised regularly to reflect current practices.

- Employees use shortcuts to perform their tasks, circumventing internal control procedures.

- Changes in organization or activities are not reflected in policies or procedures.

- Employees' duties are changed significantly in ways that may affect internal control policies.

Examining personnel should report deviations, along with an assessment of their significance, to the examiner-in-charge (EIC).

The proliferation of computer systems and personal computers (PCs) requires increased controls over computer operations. Because banks depend on computers, embezzlement or misuse of funds is often a computer crime. The list of persons whose computers have access to assets or financial records can often be long; it includes computer operators, programmers, their supervisors, and others. Banks should impose sophisticated controls not only on mainframe operations but also on the systems and records maintained on

---

[4] For additional information on conflicts of interest, refer to the "Insider Activities" booklet of the Comptroller's Handbook.

PCs, local area networks (LANs), and wide area networks (WANs). Controls on these systems are of paramount importance; examiners should refer to the Federal Financial Institutions Examination Council Information System Examination Handbook for further details on such controls.

Controls over information processing, whether automated or manual, should be adequate to ensure the integrity of management information systems, books, and records. Bank employees should enter pertinent information into processing systems in a timely manner, and appropriate bank personnel should independently test that information for accuracy. Bank personnel should maintain trial balances and subsidiary ledgers and reconcile those ledgers to general ledgers in a timely manner, investigate and resolve any differences noted, and ensure appropriate personnel review and approve completed reconcilements in a timely manner. Procedures should also exist to test the accuracy of spreadsheets and reports created by individual users.

At the conclusion of the control review or other targeted reviews, examiners should give the EIC written narrative comments on significant findings, both positive and negative, about the control system. The EIC uses these findings to determine how the quality of the control system affects the bank's risk management system. In the long run, internal control findings and comments also help examiners establish and maintain core knowledge about a bank.

A significant deficiency in a control system is a deficiency in risk management. For example, the failure to process transactions in an accurate, thorough, and timely manner (a failure of internal control) exposes the bank to potential losses (transaction risk). Other examples of such deficiencies are inadequate underwriting standards and failure to follow established underwriting standards, both of which expose the bank to credit risk losses. Such failures may lead to compliance errors, inaccurate management information systems, material misstatements in financial statements, and employee fraud that expose the bank to strategic and reputation risks.

Examiners should fully document specific weaknesses, as well as recommendations on how to correct them. Doing so facilitates their review and incorporation in the report of examination. The EIC should discuss significant weaknesses or recommendations with bank management. Serious weaknesses should be communicated directly to the board of directors or audit committee. For banks with serious control weaknesses, EICs should determine whether to recommend that the appropriate supervisory office (1) direct bank management to develop a safety and soundness compliance plan as outlined in 12 CFR 30 or (2) take other supervisory action to address noted issues and concerns. In making its decision, the supervisory office considers the significance of the weaknesses, management's ability and commitment to effect corrective action, and the risks posed to the bank's safety and soundness.

Board and Management Oversight

The hallmark of a positive control environment is a commitment by the board of directors and senior management to strong controls. A bank's board of directors and management are responsible for establishing and maintaining effective internal control that meets statutory and regulatory requirements and responds to changes in the bank's environment and conditions. They must ensure that the system operates as intended and is modified appropriately when circumstances dictate. The board and management must make sure that the bank's information systems produce pertinent and timely information in a form that enables employees, auditors, and examiners to carry out their respective responsibilities.

The board of directors, which oversees the control system in general, approves and reviews the business strategies and policies that govern the system. They are also responsible for understanding risk limits and setting acceptable ones for the bank's major business activities, establishing organizational control structure, and making sure senior management identifies, measures, monitors, and controls risks and monitors internal control effectiveness. The board should (1) discuss periodically the internal control system's effectiveness with management; (2) review internal control evaluations conducted by management, auditors, and examiners in a timely manner; (3) monitor management's actions on auditor and examiner internal control recommendations and concerns; and (4) periodically review the bank's strategy and risk limits. In some banks, the board of directors delegates these duties and responsibilities to an audit committee, risk committee, or both.

Senior management oversees operations and provides leadership and direction for the communication and monitoring of control policies, practices, and processes. They implement the board's strategies and policies by establishing effective internal control and delegating or allocating control duties and responsibilities to appropriate personnel. Management is also responsible for performing background checks on staff members before they are hired and ensuring that they are qualified, experienced, trained, and compensated to effectively conduct control activities.

Board and management must consider whether a control system's methods, records, and procedures are proper in relation to the bank's

- Asset size.
- Organization and ownership characteristics.
- Business activities.
- Operational complexity.
- Risk profile.
- Methods of processing data.
- Legal and regulatory requirements.

The board of directors must ensure that management properly considers the risks and control issues of emerging technologies, enhanced information systems, and electronic banking. These issues include: more users with access to information systems; less segregated duties; a shift from paper to electronic audit trails; a lack of standards and controls for end-user systems; and, more complex contingency planning and recovery planning for information systems.

Examination Procedures

These procedures will help an examiner determine the quality and reliability of the bank's policies, procedures, and processes with respect to internal control functions. Examiners do not have to perform all the procedures or perform the procedures strictly in the order presented, but they should fit the procedures to the bank's circumstances and the examination objectives. Evaluating a bank's internal control functions involves assessing control functions and processes of the bank as a whole, as well as specific bank activities and operations. The review of internal control should be closely coordinated with the reviews of other areas of the bank (e.g., audit, credit, capital markets, compliance, and information systems). Coordination can reduce burden on the bank, prevent duplication of examination efforts, and be an effective cross-check of the bank's compliance and process integrity.

These examination procedures supplement the minimum core assessment control objectives in the "Community Bank Supervision" and "Large Bank Supervision" booklets of the Comptroller's Handbook. Examiners should begin their internal control reviews with the minimum objectives and steps from those sections. The examiner's assessment of risk, the supervisory strategy objectives, and any examination scope memorandum should determine which of this booklet's procedural and validation steps to perform to meet examination objectives. Seldom will every objective/step of this booklet's procedures be required to satisfy examination objectives.

Planning the Control Review

Objective: Determine the scope and objectives of the examination of internal control.

1.   Obtain and review the following documents to identify any previous problems that require follow-up. Consider

☐ Previous reports of examination, conclusion memorandum of targeted reviews or on-going activities, and key supervisory information (e.g., strategy, analyses, and other significant events) in OCC databases.

☐ EIC's scope memorandum, if applicable.

☐ OCC internal control summary memos and work papers from the previous examination.

☐ Internal and external audit reports, including any management assertions and independent public accountant attestations on internal control.

☐ Workpapers prepared by management to support their 12 CFR 363 annual internal control assertion.

☐ Minutes of any audit committees and applicable board of directors' minutes since the last examination.

☐ Correspondence memorandum.

☐ List of claims filed with bonding company since the previous safety and soundness examination.

☐ Information on operational losses sustained during the past 12 months.

Note: The "CEO Questionnaire – Internal Control and Audit" (appendix A) may help examiners perform step 2.

2. Determine during early discussion with management or through on-going activities:

- How management supervises internal control activities.
- Any significant changes in business strategy or activities that could affect internal control.
- Any material changes in the internal control functions.
- Any other internal or external factors that could affect or may have affected the internal control function.

3. Obtain from management, the internal auditor, or the examiner responsible for audit review a list of all significant outstanding internal control deficiencies noted in audit reports. Determine whether

management has corrected deficiencies and, if not, determine the reason why corrective action has not been initiated. Consider

- Distributing to each examiner responsible for an examination area a copy of significant internal control deficiencies in that area.

- Requesting that the examiner prepare and return a memorandum stating whether the board or management has addressed the internal control deficiencies and whether their actions were adequate.

- Assessing management's ability and desire to implement corrective actions.

4.   Using findings from the preceding steps and OCC's review of internal audit, determine how much to rely on the bank's assessments of internal control. Consider

- Consulting with the EIC to determine how thoroughly internal control should be tested or verified.

- Coordinating validation with examiners responsible for reviewing the bank's functional or specialty areas (e.g., credit, capital markets, compliance, information systems, and fiduciary).

5.   Determine the scope of the examination and select additional procedures, including ICQs and verification procedures, as appropriate.

Conclusion: The quality of internal control is (strong, satisfactory, weak).

Note: Examiners should use appropriate tools (e.g., the CEO questionnaire, ICQs, and FDICIA internal control assertion work papers) and findings from all areas under examination, including the OCC's review of the bank's audit functions, when completing these objectives and steps.

When substantive supervisory concerns about the adequacy of internal control or the integrity of financial reporting controls exist after achieving the following objectives and performing the following steps, examiners should consider performing additional examination procedures, such as using ICQs, for those areas of concern. If, after completing those additional procedures, examiners remain concerned about internal control adequacy or financial reporting control integrity, they should perform appropriate verification procedures to confirm the existence and description of bank assets. As an alternative, examiners may require the bank to expand its own verification program to include the areas of weakness or deficiency; however, this alternative will be used only if management has demonstrated a capacity and willingness to address regulatory problems, if there are no concerns about management's integrity, and if management has initiated timely corrective action in the past. Use of this alternative must result in timely resolution of each identified supervisory problem. If examiners use this alternative, supervisory follow-up must include a review of work papers in areas where the bank's program was expanded.

Control Environment

Objective: Determine whether the institution's control environment embodies the principles of strong internal control.

1. Assess the effectiveness of the control environment. Consider

   • The integrity, ethics, and competence of personnel.

- The organizational structure of the institution.
- Management's philosophy and operating style.
- External influences affecting operations and practices.
- Personnel policies and practices.
- The attention and direction provided by the board of directors and its committees, especially the audit or risk management committees.

2. Determine whether the board periodically reviews policies and procedures to ensure that proper risk assessment and control processes have been instituted.

3. Determine whether there is an audit or other control system in place to periodically test and monitor compliance with internal control policies/procedures and to report to the board instances of noncompliance.

    - Does the board review the qualifications and independence of internal and external auditors?

    - Do auditors report their findings directly to the board or its audit committee?

    - Does the board take appropriate follow-up action when instances of noncompliance are reported?

4. Determine whether management provides the board and its representatives complete access to bank records.

5. Determine whether board decisions are made collectively or whether dominant individuals control those decisions.

6. Determine whether management information systems provide the board information they need to make informed and timely decisions.

7. Determine whether the board receives adequate information about the bank's internal risk assessment process.

8. Determine whether the board or management communicates policies regarding the importance of internal control and appropriate conduct to all employees.

9. Determine whether codes of conduct or ethics policies exist.

   • Do audit or other control systems exist to periodically test for compliance with codes of conduct or ethics policies?

   • Do audit or other control system personnel routinely review policies and training regarding ethics or codes of conduct?

Risk Assessment

Objective: Determine whether the institution's risk assessment system allows the board and management to plan for and respond to existing and emerging risks in the institution's activities.

1. Determine whether the board and management involve audit personnel or other internal control experts in the risk assessment and risk evaluation process.

2. Determine whether the risk assessment/evaluation process involves sufficient staff members who are competent, knowledgeable, and provided with adequate resources.

3. Determine whether the board and management discuss and appropriately evaluate risks and consider control issues during the pre-planning stages for new products and activities.

4. Determine whether audit personnel or other internal control experts are involved when the bank is developing new products and activities.

5. Determine whether the board and management consider and appropriately address technology issues.

6. Determine the adequacy of blanket bond or other risk insurance coverage in relation to the bank's risk profile.

Control Activities

Objective: Determine whether the board and senior management have established effective control activities in all lines of business.

1. Determine whether policies and procedures exist to ensure that decisions are made with appropriate approvals and authorizations for transactions and activities.

2. Determine whether processes exist to ensure that

   - The performance and integrity of each function (e.g., lending, wire transfer) are independently checked and verified using an appropriate sample of transactions.

   - Accounts are reconciled continually, independently, and in a timely manner and that outstanding items, both on- and off-balance-sheet, are resolved and cleared.

   - Policy overrides are minimal and exceptions are reported to management.

   - Employees in sensitive positions or risk-taking activities do not have absolute control over areas. For example,

     - Is there segregation or rotation of duties to ensure that the same employee does not originate a transaction, process it, and reconcile it to the general ledger account?

     - Is there periodic unannounced rotation of duties for employees or vacation requirements that ensure their absence for at least a two-week period?

     - Are safeguards in place for access to and use of sensitive assets and records, including wire transfer activities?

    – Is there dual control or joint custody over access to assets (e.g., cash, negotiable collateral, official checks, or consigned items)?

3.   Determine whether reporting lines within a business or functional area provide sufficient independence of the control function.

- Is separation of duties emphasized in the organizational structure?

- Are systems in place to ensure that personnel abide by separation of duty requirements?

- Is there supervision and oversight of payments against uncollected funds (potential for kiting)?

- Is there an internal review of employee accounts and expense reports?

- Are personnel accountable for the actions they take and the responsibilities/authorities given to them?

4.   Determine whether operating practices conflict with established areas of responsibility and control. Examiners should

- Interview line and management personnel.
- Review policies delineating responsibilities.
- Review reconciliations and transaction origination.
- Reviews internal audit work papers.
- Review external audit reports.

5.   Determine whether internal audit or other control review functions are sufficiently independent. Consider:

- Where the function reports, administratively, within the organization.

- To whom, or to what level, the function reports the results of work performed.

- Whether practices conform to established standards.

- Whether management unduly influences the timeliness of risk analysis and control processes.

6.   Determine whether the board and senior management has established adequate procedures for ensuring compliance with applicable laws and regulations. Examiners should

- Determine the frequency of testing and reporting for compliance with laws and regulations by reviewing:

  – Audit schedules, scopes, and reports.
  – Minutes of senior management and board committees.
  – The payment of any fines or liabilities arising from litigation against the institution or its employees.

- Determine whether appropriate attention and follow-up are given to violations of laws and regulations. Consider:

  – The significance and frequency of the violations.
  – The willingness and ability to prevent reoccurrence.

Accounting, Information, and Communication Systems

Objective: Determine whether the institution's accounting, information, and communication systems ensure that risk-taking activities are within policy guidelines and that the systems are adequately tested and reviewed.

1.   Assess the adequacy of accounting systems by determining whether

- The systems properly identify, assemble, analyze, classify, record, and report the institution's transactions in accordance with GAAP.

- The systems account for all assets and liabilities involved in transactions.

2. Assess the adequacy of information systems by determining

   - The type, number, and depth of reports generated for operational, financial, managerial, and compliance-related activities.

   - Whether reports are sufficient to properly run and control the institution.

   - Whether access to information systems is properly restricted.

3. Assess the adequacy of communication systems by determining whether

   - Significant information is imparted throughout the institution (from the top down and from the bottom up in the organizational chain), ensuring that personnel understand:

     - Their roles in the control system.
     - How their activities relate to others.
     - Their accountability for the activities they conduct.

   - Significant information is imparted to external parties such as regulators, shareholders, and customers.

4. Assess how frequently and thoroughly the accounting, information, and communication systems are verified. Consider:

   - The frequency of testing given the level of risk and sophistication of the systems.

   - The sufficiency of ongoing reviews of the systems' accuracy.

   - The competency, knowledge, and independence of the personnel doing the testing.

- The sufficiency of contingency planning.

Self-assessment and Monitoring

Objective: Determine whether senior management and the board properly oversee internal control, control reviews, and audit findings.

1. Determine whether the board or a designated board committee has reviewed management's actions to deal with material control weaknesses and verified that corrective actions are objective and adequate. Consider:

    - Minutes of appropriate board and committee meetings.
    - Audit or other control review reports and follow-up reports.

2. Determine the frequency and comprehensiveness of reports to the board or board committee and senior management:

    - Review the minutes of appropriate board or committee meetings.

    - Determine whether the reports are sufficiently detailed.

    - Determine whether reports are presented in a timely manner to allow for resolution and appropriate action.

3. Determine the adequacy of the board's or board committee's review of audit and other control functions. Consider whether the board or its committee

    - Reviewed the qualifications and independence of personnel evaluating controls (e.g., external auditors, internal auditors, or line managers).

    - Approved the overall scope of control review activities (e.g., audit, loan review, etc.).

    - Reviewed the results of control evaluations.

- Approved the system of internal control.

- Periodically reviews the adequacy of audit or other control systems.

4. Assess the adequacy and independence of the audit or other control review function. Consider:

- Results of audit's or other control review function's control evaluation and supporting work papers.

- The function's organizational structure and reporting lines.

- The scope and frequency of audits or reviews for all lines of business.

- Audit or control review reports, management responses, and follow-up reports.

5. Determine whether management responses to audit or other control review findings are fully documented and tracked for adequate follow-up. Consider whether

- Documentation detailing the coverage, findings, and follow-up of control weaknesses is adequate.

- Management gives appropriate and timely attention to material control weaknesses once identified.

- Line management is held accountable for unsatisfactorily or ineffectively following up on control weaknesses.

Statutory Requirements

Objective: Using the findings from the preceding objectives and steps, determine compliance with 12 CFR 30, 12 CFR 363, and 15 USC 78m, the statutory requirements for internal control.

12 CFR 30, Safety and Soundness Standards

1. Determine whether the bank has internal control and information systems that are appropriate to its size and the nature, scope, and risk of its activities. Determine whether the system complies with 12 CFR 30, appendix A, "Operational and Managerial Standards," in providing for:

   • An organizational structure that establishes clear lines of authority and responsibility for monitoring adherence to established policies.

   • Effective risk assessment.

   • Timely and accurate financial, operational, and regulatory reports.

   • Adequate procedures to safeguard and manage assets.

   • Compliance with applicable laws and regulations.

2. If the bank fails to meet these standards, contact the supervisory office and discuss recommendation to:

   • Have bank management develop a safety and soundness compliance plan as outlined in 12 CFR 30,

   • Issue the bank a safety and soundness order, or

   • Take other supervisory action, as appropriate.

12 CFR 363, Audit, Reporting, and Audit Committees

NOTE: These steps are applicable for all national banks with total assets of $500 million or more.

1. Determine whether the bank has prepared a management report, as of its most recent fiscal year end, that is signed by its chief executive officer and chief accounting or chief financial officer (12 CFR 363.2(b)).

2. Determine whether the management report contained:

    - A statement of management's responsibilities

        - To prepare the institution's annual financial statements.
        - To establish and maintain adequate internal control and procedures for financial reporting.
        - To comply with laws and regulations relating to safety and soundness which are designated by the OCC (12 CFR 363.2(b)(1)).

    - Management's assessments of

        - The effectiveness of internal control and procedures as of the end of its fiscal year.
        - The institution's compliance with laws and regulations during the fiscal year (12 CFR 363.2(b)(2)).

3. Determine whether the institution engaged an independent public accountant (IPA) who, in accordance with generally accepted standards for attestation engagements (GASAE), examined, attested to, and reported separately on management's assertions concerning internal control and procedures for financial reporting (12 CFR 363.3(b)).

4. Determine whether management has performed its own investigation and review for compliance with designated laws (12 CFR 363, appendix A, table 1).

5.	For banks that fail to comply with these requirements, consider stepped-up supervisory or enforcement action designed to achieve compliance.

15 USC 78m, Securities Exchange Act of 1934

NOTE: These steps are applicable to all national banks that have registered securities.

1.	Determine whether the bank makes and keeps books, records, and accounts that, in reasonable detail, accurately and fairly reflect its transactions and dispositions of assets.

2.	Determine whether the bank has established and maintains a system of internal accounting controls sufficient to provide reasonable assurances that

- Transactions are executed in accordance with management's general or specific authorizations.

- Transactions are recorded as necessary

  - To permit preparation of financial statements in conformance with generally accepted accounting principles or any other criteria applicable to such statements, and

  - To ensure that the bank can account for assets.

- Access to assets is permitted only in accordance with management's general or specific authorizations.

- Recorded accounts of assets are compared with actual assets at reasonable intervals and appropriate action is taken to reconcile any differences.

3.   For banks that fail to comply with these requirements, consider stepped-up supervisory or enforcement action designed to achieve compliance. Also, consider whether referral to the SEC is appropriate.

Overall Conclusions

Conclusion: The institution's internal control is (strong, satisfactory, weak)

Objective: Assess the overall effectiveness and adequacy of the institution's internal control, communicate findings to the EIC, management, and the board of directors, and complete/update OCC work papers.

1. Prepare written conclusion summaries, discuss findings with the EIC, and communicate findings to management. Conclusion summaries should address, as appropriate,

   • Whether the internal control environment poses actual or potential undue risk to the institution's financial performance for any of the following reasons:

     − The magnitude of control exceptions.
     − Financial effect of inaccurate, untimely, or improper transactions.
     − Previous losses from fraud.
     − Claims against insurance policies.
     − Employee turnover.
     − Other high operational losses.
     − Violations of laws or regulations and nonconformance with established internal policies and procedures related to the internal control functions.

   • The adequacy of internal control policies, procedures, and programs to control and limit risk in bank operations.

   • Whether bank personnel operate in conformance with established policies and, if not, the causes and consequences of nonconformance.

   • The adequacy of information on the internal control function received by the board or its committees and management.

- Significant areas of control weakness identified by internal or external audits or other control reviews and the board's and management's progress in addressing those weaknesses.

- Audit or other control review report findings not acted upon by management, as well as any other concerns or recommendations resulting from the review of internal control functions.

- Recommended corrective actions, if applicable, and management's commitments.

2. Determine how the quality of internal control affects the aggregate level and direction of OCC risk assessments. Examiners should refer to guidance provided under the OCC's risk assessment programs for large and community banks.

3. Determine how the quality of internal control affects the bank's composite and component CAMELS ratings. In coordination with examiners performing information system/technology, asset management, and fiduciary reviews, communicate the effect of control findings and conclusions on Uniform Rating System for Information Technology (URSIT), Uniform Interagency Trust Rating System (UITRS), and compliance ratings.

4. Determine, in consultation with the EIC, whether the risks identified are significant enough to merit bringing them to the board's attention in the report of examination.

   If so, prepare items for inclusion under the heading "Matters Requiring Attention" (MRA). MRA comments should cover practices that (1) deviate from sound fundamental principles and are likely to result in financial deterioration if not addressed or (2) result in substantive noncompliance with laws or internal policies or processes. The examiner should provide details regarding:

   - Factors contributing to the problem.
   - Consequences of inaction.

- Management's commitment to corrective action.
- The time frame for any corrective action and who is responsible for the action.

5.   Update any applicable schedule or table and include a comment on internal control in the report of examination. The comment should address

- Adequacy of internal control policies and processes, internal control and overall programs, personnel, and board oversight.

- Significant problems discerned by the auditors or other control reviewers that have not been corrected.

- Any deficiencies or concerns reviewed with management, any corrective actions recommended by examiners, and management commitments to corrective actions.

6.   Prepare a memorandum and update OCC work programs with any information that will facilitate future examinations. Make recommendations about the scope of the next internal control review and determine whether internal control findings should change the scopes of other area reviews.

7.   Update the OCC databases, including rating screens/schedules.

8.   Organize and reference work papers in accordance with PPM 5400-8, "Examination Work Papers."

Appendix A: CEO Questionnaire – Internal Control and Audit

This questionnaire will help examiners obtain preliminary information about the bank's formal or informal internal control and monitoring procedures. Depending on the specific characteristics of the bank, the examiner may add or delete questions as warranted. Use of this questionnaire is encouraged, but is not mandatory and can be used at the EIC's discretion.

Examiners should meet with the bank's chief executive officer (CEO), or the person most directly responsible for internal control if not the CEO, to conduct informal discussions on board and management oversight, segregation of duties, dual control, employee policies, and audit functions. Examiners are encouraged to obtain and review appropriate reports and other information that substantiate management's assertions on internal control (e.g., audit engagement letters, internal and external audit reports and management letters/responses, board reports, organizational charts, and policy/procedural manuals).

Board and Management Oversight

1. What goals and objectives have you and the board established for internal control (e.g., management oversight, dual control, rotation of duties, timing/frequency or reconciliations, internal control reviews, risk assessments, and frequency and scope of internal control audits)? Who is chiefly responsible for ensuring that those controls are adhered to? Does any one individual significantly influence board decisions or control activities?

2. What accounting and information systems are in place to account for transactions, assets, and liabilities and ensure that risk-taking activities are within policy guidelines?

3. What type of operational, financial, managerial, and compliance-related reports does the board receive concerning risk assessments and internal control? How frequently does it receive them?

4. What written board-approved policies and procedures addressing internal control, risk assessments, and ethics/conduct are in place?

Who monitors compliance with internal control policies and procedures? Who performs risk assessments? What issues have been noted within the last 12 months?

5.   Do the board and its representatives have complete access to bank records?

6.   How do you establish what are the proper controls for new or significantly revised products, services, or operational procedures? How do you evaluate the risks associated with planned or potential new products or activities or changes to existing products or activities? Are audit or other control review personnel involved when discussing such products or activities? How are technology issues and risks considered and addressed?

7.   What new or significantly revised products, services, or operational procedures have you introduced since the last examination? What do you anticipate introducing within the next 12 months?

8.   What are the most significant risks facing the bank today? What processes do you have in place to assess and control those risks?

Control Policies, Procedures, and Activities

9.   In general, describe your internal control process for ensuring segregation and rotation of duties. Are these applied bank-wide, to all operational areas? If not, why not?

10.   How do you ensure that the same employee does not originate a transaction, process it, and reconcile the general ledger account? How are approval authorities put in place, communicated to employees, and periodically tested?

11.   How often does someone independent of a specific function or department review reconciliations and other pertinent internal control to ensure that (1) reconciliations are timely and performed by an appropriate person, (2) stale items are being researched for disposition, and (3) old items are charged off in a timely manner?

---

12. In general, describe your dual control process over the bank's cash, cash collateral, official checks, and consigned items.

13. How do you ensure you have trained and qualified employees, including back-up employees, for all risk-taking activities and positions in the bank?

14. Do you have employee policies/procedures that assist in detecting breaches of internal control (e.g., pre-employment criminal background investigation, vacation policies, rotation of duty policies, frequency of obtaining employee credit reports, sampling employee accounts, and reporting of policy overrides/exceptions)?

15. How do you communicate to employees, and do they understand, their roles in the control system, how their activities relate to others, and their accountability for the activities they conduct?

Audits

16. How does the board review qualifications and independence of internal and external auditors?

Internal Audit

17. Does the bank have an internal audit or other control review function?

18. Are any internal audit activities outsourced to another party? To whom? How are outsourced arrangements and activities supervised and managed?

19. Describe the internal auditor's educational background and experience. Who approves the hiring of key internal audit personnel?

20. What other duties does the internal auditor perform?

21. To whom does the internal auditor report? Who completes the internal auditor's annual evaluation?

22.	Describe the scope and frequency of internal audits.

23.	Does the audit scope include an assessment of risk and internal control? Is compliance with established ethics/conduct policies periodically tested?

24.	Who reviews the internal audit report (department or line manager, senior management, audit committee, board)? How frequent are reports and follow-up reviews? How do you ensure that the board or management is able to understand and act on findings? Who follows up on deficiencies (department or line manager, internal auditor, Audit Committee)? What tests ensure that corrective action has been implemented? Who does the testing?

External Audit

25.	Which of the following types of external audits does the bank receive:

*	Opinion audit (full financial statements).
*	Attestation report on internal control.
*	Opinion audit (balance sheet only).
*	Agreed-upon procedures (i.e., director's exam).

26.	Who performs the bank's external audit (independent public accountant or other independent party) and how long have they been doing the bank's audit work? What was the cost of the most recent audit? What non-audit services does the external auditor or other outside party provide for the bank? What are the fees for these services?

27.	Describe the scope and frequency of external audits and non-audit services.

28.	Is the opinion audit performed to GAAS standards? Is the report on internal control performed to attestation standards? For non-opinion audits or internal control attestation engagements, does the scope specifically include an assessment and testing of financial reporting controls or other internal control? If so, who decides which control functions will be tested and validated?

29. Who receives and reviews the external audit report or other reports issued by the external auditor (audit committee or board)? How frequent are reports and follow-up reviews? Are reports sufficiently detailed to allow the board or management to understand and act on findings? Who follows up on deficiencies (department head/line manager, auditor, audit committee, etc.)? What tests ensure that corrective action has been implemented? Who does the testing?

30. Who determines whether the external audit scope and frequency are adequate? Who ensures that the bank received what they contracted for? In other words, who ensures that the audit embodies what is in the engagement letter, specifically in the statement of scope?

CEO Self-Assessment

31. Would you rate your overall internal control and monitoring procedures strong, satisfactory, or weak?

EIC Assessment

32. Is your preliminary assessment of the bank's overall internal control that it is strong, satisfactory, or weak?

33. What areas do you think exhibit the most operational risk given the bank's internal control environment, culture, and characteristics?

34. What areas do you think exhibit the least operational risk given the bank's internal control environment, culture, and characteristics?

References

Laws

12 USC 1831m, Early Identification of Needed Improvements in Financial Management
12 USC 1831p-1, Standards for Safety and Soundness
15 USC 78m, Periodical and Other Reports

Regulations

12 CFR 30, Safety and Soundness Standards
12 CFR 363, Annual Independent Audits and Reporting Requirements

Issuances

Federal Financial Institutions Examination Council, Information Systems Examination Handbook
OCC 96-39, "Data Communications Networks, Risks, and Control Systems"
OCC Advisory Letter 2000-6, "Audit and Internal Controls"
OCC PPM 5310-10, "Guidance to Examiners in Securing Access to Bank Books and Records"

Industry Reference Sources

American Institute of Certified Public Accountants' AICPA Audit and Accounting Guide, Banks and Savings Institutions

AICPA Statement on Auditing Standards (SAS)
SAS 55, "Consideration of the Internal Control Structure in a Financial Statement Audit"
SAS 60, "Communication of Internal Control Structure Related Matters Noted in an Audit"
SAS 70, "Reports on the Processing of Transactions by Servicing Organizations"
SAS 78, "Consideration of Internal Control in a Financial Statement Audit: An Amendment to SAS 55"

Basle Committee on Banking Supervision, Framework for Internal Control Systems in Banking Organizations

Committee of Sponsoring Organizations of the Treadway Commission (COSO), Internal Control — Integrated Framework; Volume 1, Executive Summary; Volume 2, Framework; Volume 3, Reporting to External Parties; Volume 4, Evaluation Tools

Deloitte Touche Tohmatsu International, Internal Audit in Leading Financial Institutions

Ernst and Young, Evaluating Internal Control. Three booklets: "A Guide for Management," "Assessment of the Control Environment: Documentation Supplement," and "Application Evaluations: Documentation Supplements"

The Institute of Internal Auditors, Control Self-Assessment: Making the Choice

Web Sites
AICPA (www.aicpa.org)
Bank Administration Institute (www.bai.org)
Basle Committee on Banking Supervision (www.bis.org)
Institute of Internal Auditors (www.theiia.org)